30 Minutes
... To Boost Your Self-Esteem

Patricia Cleghorn

KOGAN PAGE

First Indian Edition 2003
Reprinted 2008

Kogan Page India Private Limited
4737/23 Ansari Road,
Daryaganj
New Delhi 110 002

ISBN-10: 81-7554-212-8
ISBN-13: 978-81-7554-212-9

Published by Vinod Vasishtha for Kogan Page India Private Limited, 4737/23 Ansari Road, Daryaganj, New Delhi - 110 002.

Printed and bound at Print Perfect, New Delhi - 110 064.

CONTENTS

The 30 Minutes Series

The Kogan Page 30 Minutes Series has been devised to give your confidence a boost when faced with tackling a new skill or challenge for the first time.

So the next time you're thrown in at the deep end and want to bring your skills up to scratch or pep up your career prospects, turn to the *30 Minutes Series* for help!

Titles available are:
30 Minutes Before A Meeting
30 Minutes Before A Presentation
30 Minutes to Boost Your Communication Skills
30 Minutes to Boost Your Self Esteem
30 Minutes to Brainstorm Great Ideas
30 Minutes to Deal With Difficult People
30 Minutes to Get Your Own Way
30 Minutes to Get Promoted
30 Minutes to Improve Your Networking Skills
30 Minutes to Make the Right Decision
30 Minutes to Manage Your Time Better
30 Minutes to Market Yourself
30 Minutes to Master the Internet
30 Minutes to Motivate Your Staff
30 Minutes to Negotiate a Better Deal
30 Minutes to Plan a Project
30 Minutes to Solve that Problem
30 Minutes to Succeed in Business Writing
30 Minutes to Write a Business Plan
30 Minutes to Write a Marketing Plan
30 Minutes to Write a Report
30 Minutes to Write Sales Letters

Available from all good bookseller.
For further information on the series, please contact:

INTRODUCTION

Self-esteem is not a quality bestowed on the lucky few, with everyone else left in the lurch with low self-esteem. Self-confidence can be built. You can learn to boost your own self-esteem. While you may usefully spend a longer time to work out for yourself what makes you feel good, here are some tried and tested approaches which I and my tutors have used over the years with hundreds of people. These will save you time!

It is wonderful if you have a boss who has the time and knowledge to help build the self-esteem of each member of staff. This doesn't happen very often, particularly nowadays when everything is happening so quickly and with increased demands on everyone at work. You may even be the boss, with little idea of how to boost your own self-esteem when the pressure is on, far less anyone else's. You may be one of many thousands in your organization, feeling like a small cog in a large wheel.

With so many people at all levels feeling over-worked and under-valued, it's an *important career skill to be able to boost your own self-esteem. As well as feeling much more confident when you do this, it will motivate you and help you feel back in control of your working life.*

It's excellent to want to know how to boost your self-esteem – you have already realized the importance of feeling good about yourself. The key to success and satisfaction not only lies within you but you are the only one that can make the necessary changes in the way you think about yourself. *The power and authority in your life lie with you.* This is regardless of your current circumstances, of whether there is a bad atmosphere at work or one that is making too many demands on you.

Never give up or feel you can't make changes or that you haven't time. Even if you have only a short time to spend, you can boost your self-esteem. You may read the book through or dip into it to choose a way of boosting your self-esteem.

This book is designed to be used when time is short and you're feeling low or when you want that extra edge and sparkle.

1

TAKE A MINUTE TO . . .

Consider Your True Worth

Self-value

How much do you really value yourself? Do you sometimes feel under-valued and unappreciated? Are there times and situations when you feel lacking in self-worth? Would you like to feel inwardly confident instead of struggling to maintain an outward facade of confidence?

Perhaps more than anything, you want to have a way of giving that confidence to yourself when the pressure is on and you're short of time. So now if you simply let go and take a few minutes, you can start to build a basis of self-esteem that will assist you in moving forward.

Handle self-criticism

You know how unpleasant and how unhelpful it is and how much you dislike it when you're the object of another person's criticism. We're not talking about recommendations at work that will save you time and increase your options, we're talking about carping, insulting remarks, that leave our self-esteem in tatters. Although we may not stand for this from other people, *we often subject ourselves to self-criticism of the very worst kind.* This sort of self-criticism wears you down day after day.

You may feel think 'Oh, it's only words'. *Words are very powerful whether spoken out loud or to yourself.* They have an effect, particularly on you! When other people say something critical about you, you feel angry, put down and yet you can be very capable of putting yourself down. We do this by the thoughts in our heads and by speaking the words out loud to ourselves and others – that is, by going on a self-critical binge.

Appreciate yourself

By the same token you can perk yourself up! That's where your power comes in, your self-esteem, both in letting go of and refusing to continue entertaining these self-critical thoughts and in deliberately looking for things to appreciate about yourself, things that you *are* doing right. Even on a simple level, at the end of each day before you leave your office or place of work, instead of berating yourself for all the things you haven't done or didn't do well, focus on what you have achieved, what you *are* doing well.

How often have you heard people at work say 'I wish they would just show some appreciation', 'I feel like rubbish', 'No-one ever thanks me for the hard graft I put in'? As you may often feel unappreciated in your workplace, you need to be able to give yourself a boost by appreciating yourself. Once you've achieved a task, stop and appreciate how well you are doing, how far you have come, before you go on to the next piece of work and remember to express your appreciation to others.

It is a matter of focus. You are powerful, in charge, because you decide what you want to focus on.

What are three things you have done well or achieved today?

Remember to ask yourself this at the end of each day. Write down your achievements so they can form the basis of your success list!

It's so easy to be critical because it's a habit. Yet you can establish the habit of appreciating yourself instead. Think of the times you've been self-critical today, view these as opportunities to appreciate yourself instead. Notice where you can be more appreciative:

What is one thing you like/appreciate about:
Your body and appearance?
Your attitude to a challenge?
The way you relate to others?
Your contribution at work?

Write down your answers so you can remind yourself of these good points. Each time you find yourself thinking of something you don't like about yourself, also deliberately find something you *do* like. Again write this down, you can look back at these appreciations of yourself next time you're feeling low and add to your appreciation list.

Self-acceptance

While we may want to change and improve ourselves or aspects of our lives, it's still possible and desirable to *appreciate* and accept ourselves as we are *right now*. There will always be aspects that we will want to change and improve. However, you are still worthy of experiencing self-esteem rather than non-acceptance of yourself. In fact, while you won't accept yourself and therefore constantly discourage yourself, your progress is likely to be slow and less pleasant than it could be!

So to boost your self-esteem, set out to make these changes in a spirit of joyful co-operation with yourself. You'll find it easier, quicker and more enjoyable with your own support.

Approve of yourself

Approval – self-approval – is a strong constituent of self-esteem. While at work, for example, you may need to have a proposal approved by your boss or supervisor. This is different from constantly needing the approval of others. Do you often find yourself feeling you have to justify your desires, choices, preferences? Do you provide explanations for these to other people when really it's none of their business? Do you feel disapproved of by others, that they are judgemental of you?

In the course of growing up, a fair amount of disapproval comes our way from the various people in our lives who are 'responsible' for us when we are young. Even though no lasting disapproval is intended, it is easy to see how this happens when we're told 'Oh, you're so lazy', 'don't do that, do this instead', 'you shouldn't', 'you always', 'couldn't you have done better than that?' And so the individual, understandably, feels disapproved of. Not only that, there's a tendency then to feel unworthy and to add your own disapproval of yourself to the chorus, saying to yourself statements like 'I'm so lazy', 'Oh, you fool you should have ...', whether you say these out loud or repeat them to yourself in your head.

An otherwise excellent manager was spending too much time and energy by being overly concerned with whether his boss approved of him. He was able to progress rapidly when he had his own self-approval and gave himself permission to move forward.

Remember, the person whose approval you so badly want may be wanting *your approval!* Constantly comparing yourself to others, wasting energy on that, will create self-disapproval rather than self-approval. The antidote to all this disapproval is lots of approval! So *really start now to step up your level of self-approval.*

- What is one situation where it would help you to have more self-approval?
- Who do you feel you need more self-approval with?
- Is there a work-related situation where it would help you to have more self-approval?
- What about at home with your family or friends?
- Are there other times, perhaps socially, when more self-approval will help you?

Identify these times, writing them down so you can refer to them to bring in more approval of yourself, for example before being with a particular person and while you are with them. Do the same with the other situations that you have considered.

Give yourself permission to move forward

Giving yourself permission is also part of self-approval. Notice if there are things you are holding back on. This may be in relation to what you would love to do because they would be enjoyable. Perhaps you are pressuring yourself to work instead or you may feel you haven't quite enough self-approval to start something new. Could you allow yourself to move forward with your own self-approval rather than waiting for that approval from anyone else? After our programmes people report that when they boost their level of self-esteem, their self-approval helps them to take on new opportunities and situations. Are there aspects of your life you are now willing to move forward?

Self-esteem boosters

- Stop self-criticism. Next time you go on a self-critical binge, don't allow yourself to continue – halt the flow of critical thoughts and even think of something you appreciate about yourself instead.
- Notice your good points and what you *are* achieving. Write them down and keep them as reminders to yourself.
- Practise accepting yourself, especially when you're feeling judgemental.
- Bring in self-approval as often as you can today, check your self-approval 'quotient' throughout the day.
- Give yourself permission to move forward in one way this week. What steps will you now take?

Keynote booster

Keynote boosters can be used for a day or more, then use another booster of your choice.

Take a minute . . . several times today to practise the three As of self-esteem:

A*ppreciate yourself,* ***A****ccept yourself and* ***A****pprove of yourself.*

2

ATTITUDE IS ALL

Do You Have The Right Attitude *To Yourself*?

Your thoughts – do they help or hinder you?

The person it is most important to have the right thoughts and attitude to is *you*. Take a moment to consider. Are your thoughts about yourself helpful? That is, do they support all you want to have, become and do? There is little point in having a goal to achieve something, whether that's gaining promotion at work or completing a qualification that will help you in your career, if you constantly tell yourself 'I'll never be able to do this' or 'I'm not good enough'.

At best, you'll make the process more difficult and more unpleasant than it need be, and at worst you'll put yourself off altogether by your low self-esteem thoughts. These thoughts can also be picked up by others, however much of an outer show of confidence and bravado you put on. And conversely when you do feel you're good enough, when you do feel good about yourself, you will still want to take the appropriate steps, yet you won't need to try so hard to impress: people will *know*.

Self-esteem thoughts for results

People at work frequently set goals and project targets. While they may deal with any logistical and strategic objections, the *thoughts* of those on their team are rarely taken into consideration. It is highly practical for everyone in a team to be aware of the power of their thoughts. With regard to your individual contribution, while taking all the practical steps you need, notice if you are telling yourself low self-esteem thoughts like 'I'm not good enough', 'I can't do this well', 'other people are doing better'. You'll slow yourself down and make the process more difficult and less enjoyable. Change these thoughts so that you remind yourself that you are good enough, you are doing well enough, also that your contribution is of value, regardless of whether this is fully appreciated.

We've seen that the most common 'downers' to your self-esteem are indulging in a self-critical 'binge', letting unhelpful thoughts go unchecked so you end up constricting your vision of yourself and the world. You remedy this by each time these 'downers' pervade your mind, you say 'stop' and make a concerted effort to choose thoughts that are helpful – 'I am good enough', 'I can handle this', 'I deserve to have this work out'.

You can choose what you want to think

So your thoughts can actually help or hinder you. Low-level, unhelpful thoughts like 'I'm not good enough', 'I can't do this', 'it's because it's me', 'someone else could do better', 'I'm not quick/intelligent/organized enough', 'I'm too ...', all these are low-level self-esteem thoughts which, when you are unguarded and repeat them often enough, will begin to make you feel like a failure. The important thing is to remember that *you always have a choice of what you want to think*.

It can be quite a revelation when you realize that your thoughts are not random things that happen to you, but that you can control your mind! You need to *want* to do this, to realize that with determination you can choose thoughts that are helpful to you. So when you realize that you're subjecting yourself to a torrent of unhelpful thinking, you can choose to stop and boost your self-esteem instead by having supportive thoughts.

With regard to relationships, if you consistently have unhelpful critical thoughts, particularly if you say them out loud about the other person, your relationship will tend to go downhill. Conversely, if you focus on what is *right* with the person, their kindness to you, for example, then that will help your relationship. *What you put your attention on tends to increase*. Your thinking can make a relationship or situation worse or better.

Choose helpful thoughts

To boost your self-esteem, let go of any unhelpful thoughts as soon as you realize you're thinking of them. Make up a more helpful thought instead. So instead of saying 'I'll never be able to do this' say 'I'm making progress with this step by step'. Instead of saying 'Oh, I'm not good enough' say '*I am good enough*'.

Fashion your thoughts to help you as an individual so that they are in line with who you are and what you want to achieve. This also contributes considerably to any group or team effort because everyone is then giving of their best in a way that is best for them. *Choosing helpful thoughts affects your whole feeling of confidence, well-being and motivation.*

Self-esteem boosters

- Emphasize *helpful* thoughts and let go of unhelpful ones, reminding yourself of the helpful ones throughout each day.
- Just see unhelpful thoughts disappearing, imagine them in your mind's eye, rub them off a board with a magic cleaner or picture them fading and disappearing.
- Take a minute when you're feeling low to write out your unhelpful thoughts, put a line through them and change them to helpful ones so that 'I'm not good enough' becomes 'I am good enough', 'I can't do this' becomes 'I can do this'.
- Turn down the volume on thoughts that don't help. Imagine helpful thoughts being repeated in a voice you find appealing.
- What would a person who wants to feel good and have certain results need to be thinking? For example, 'I'm doing very well', 'I'm successful'. Add your own thoughts.

Keynote booster

Keynote boosters can be used for a day or more, then use another booster of your choice.

Take a minute ... several times today to use the thought 'I'm good enough to ...', completing it in different ways.

3

EMOTIONS

Surely Not At Work!

Managing your emotions

Learning how to manage, that is, to integrate your emotions, is one of the most important practical lessons we can learn with regard to boosting self-esteem. Many conflicts, unspoken as well as spoken, are difficult to handle because of low self-esteem. Nothing prompts us to feel worse and to be less productive at work than feeling trapped by our own emotions. Self-doubt and defensiveness lead to fault finding, resentment, and, in business terms, low productivity. Not the best recipe for business success! If you don't feel good about yourself, your service to others isn't going to be very good either.

When you do not come from a point of self-esteem, you can find yourself embroiled in all sorts of upsets which are wasteful of your time and destructive of your energy. They can actually make you feel ill or certainly exhausted. You're likely to have experienced this with the increased pace and pressure of work nowadays. More emotions of anger and helplessness are provoked and a desperate attempt is made either to control them, often by denying them, or expressing them in an outburst.

Emotions suppressed at work are more dangerous because they're more likely to erupt. When very strenuously denied under the cover of being 'neutral' they often explode at the wrong time!

Accept *all* your feelings

Upset feelings of one member of staff or between people at work waste more time and resources than anything else. Rather than bottling up your feelings, be aware within *yourself* which emotions you're experiencing. Be aware of the discomfort you are experiencing. For example, that uncomfortable feeling in your stomach is not what you had for lunch but was caused by your reaction to what the person who you were having lunch with was saying! As far as you can, always acknowledge to yourself what you're feeling – for example, isolated, angry, sad, frustrated. Then you can decide if it's appropriate to communicate your feelings. Sometimes it is and sometimes it's not.

What *is* important is that you relax, let yourself feel your feelings, communicate, if appropriate, and take steps that you feel are important to put in place.

Remember that you cannot dictate how other people behave. While you cannot accept bad behaviour, what will help you most is to be in charge of your own emotions, to be able to feel them and let them go. The more you pretend to yourself that you're not feeling anything or that you are 'neutral', the longer these emotions will linger and the more exhausted and distracted you will feel as you suppress them. *To boost your self-esteem, accept your feelings rather than denying or suppressing them or expressing them inappropriately.*

When someone presses your buttons!

With anger and fear, when what you feel is out of proportion to the situation, three things may be occurring:

1. You may be reacting to past pain that you've not yet resolved.
2. You may be out of harmony with yourself and your life, that is, feeling bad about yourself.
3. You may feel others have not been treating you the way you feel you should be treated.

You can resolve this by gently feeling your emotions and letting them go. Get in balance by using your self-esteem booster thoughts and actions. You can change your beliefs about yourself, other people and situations. Don't put up with unkind behaviour. Treat yourself well. Notice that when others aren't able to do this, it's a reflection on them, not on you. Whatever you decide to communicate or to do, it's very important now to refocus on yourself and what is important to you.

Resentment at work or in any other area of life causes problems. Little practical work is achieved when you focus all your energy on a problem, on how much you dislike a person or the way they are behaving. Then you feel bad and find it difficult to focus on what *is* important. It can be difficult to communicate without resentment so tackling the underlying causes and feelings within yourself are important if you're to move ahead clearly.

When we feel another person is deliberately being unkind and unfair to us, it is difficult to handle. Your upset feelings affect your self-esteem and your ability to function in all areas of your life. Even when we get the person to stop or change their offending behaviour, unless we change our minds about it and raise our self-esteem, we'll still have to deal with our feelings when the next person comes along and 'does this to us' so that we feel affected in a similar way.

Letting go of hurt feelings

A big 'downer' to our self-esteem is when we short-circuit ourselves by either bottling things up and denying our feelings or saying something hurtful to the other person. Neither of these work. Before you read on, don't beat yourself up if you recognize that's what you tend to do. We do this when we allow our mind and emotions to get caught up with fears and worry over the past and the future. With repetitive negative thoughts, it is almost as though the needle is stuck on the record of an old gramophone.

Recognize when you start to do this because it can be a vicious circle. You do it when you're feeling low and stressed and that makes you feel even lower. So stop, relax, start changing your mind and raising your self-esteem. Let go. Then deliberatetly change your mind, focus on helpful thoughts and on what is important to you.

When you feel you're stressing yourself inordinately and your self-esteem is in tatters, you need to deal with the upset you're experiencing in a way that will boost your self-esteem and not make you feel worse about yourself:

1. Acknowledge to yourself your hurt feelings and see it not as a plot to hurt you but as coming from the other person's ignorance, lack of respect.
2. Let go of blaming them. To help yourself feel better and move on, each time you find yourself dwelling on the person and their behaviour, let go and focus on something better and brighter in your own life.
3. Change your own thoughts to 'I am doing well', 'I am supported', whatever thoughts you need to help you.

4. Do for yourself whatever makes you feel good, comfortable, relaxed and also move your attention from the distraction and focus on what is important to *you*.

With self-esteem you can learn to let go of hurt feelings yet communicate clearly to focus on and ask for what you want. Emotions just are, they're not right or wrong. Listen to them – they can put you in touch with what you want. Learning to give yourself what you want can dissolve your anger and any harshness towards yourself and others.

Lighten up your feelings

You can learn to bring in happy, lighter emotions when you choose. With higher self-esteem we really can be much happier more of the time. We may be used to feeling low so changing the habit requires practice. You know what it feels like when you feel good about yourself, with things that are important to you working out. Good feelings can be prompted by a visit from a friend, completing a project successfully at work, spending even a short time doing something you enjoy, or a kiss from your child. Now imagine those good feelings. Remember them. Let yourself experience them again. As part of self-esteem you can experience more happiness, joy and peace by choosing these feelings for yourself.

Self-esteem boosters

- Ask yourself daily at different times not so much 'What do I think?' but 'What am I *feeling*?' 'How do I *feel* about this?'
- Relax and feel your feelings, don't block them, they'll flow and go.

- When you are really angry, do something physical, for example 'chop a log of wood' or walk round the block. This will help to integrate emotions at least short term.
- To stop upsetting patterns repeating, let go of resentment. Ideally acknowledge your feelings then let go of blaming.
- Learn to communicate your feelings without blaming. This takes practice but it's well worth it.
- Refocus on yourself and what is important to you and gives you joy.
- Learn to bring in good feelings, remember times when you have been happy, at peace, joyful. Remember and then focus on those feelings so you can bring in the experience of them now.

Keynote booster

Keynote boosters can be used for a day or more, then use another booster of your choice.

Take a minute . . . several times today to make friends with your feelings. Enjoy your emotions or let them go.

4

HARMONY, SWEET HARMONY!

Self-Esteem For Improved Relationships At Work

Harmony begins with you. To keep your self-esteem high, and this is really the only way you can perform at an optimum level, pay attention to your interactions with others. Even when no harsh words are spoken, you can have much resentment and anger between people. So for self-esteem, 'correct' this at source by integrating your feelings, that is, acknowledging how you feel to yourself and then letting the feelings move and change.

When there is bitchiness or bullying from either sex, don't let it get you down. It's important to bring what is happening to your colleagues' attention and again this may require self-esteem. Take things as far as you can, then refocus on yourself and what is important to you rather than letting this behaviour be totally distracting to you.

In an emergency, take a deep breath, count to 10, anything that helps you stabilize and get centred. Revenge seldom works and good relationships with a colleague or a customer are required long term for a harmonious outcome that lasts. Make time to reflect, to decide what your objectives are long term. Work on your self-esteem to help you achieve this desired outcome rather than wasting your time on who is right and who is wrong.

Self-esteem for everyone

You can very often get low group self-esteem. There's no need to be affected and in fact you can raise the level of the group's self-esteem by refusing to be sucked in. Remember, *you choose*. It's so common to find everyone in a group or department or even a company moaning and groaning about how bad things are. This also lowers everyone's self-esteem, their motivation and morale.

Everyone likes to feel appreciated for their contribution and it has a wonderful effect on self-esteem. Yet appreciation is rarely expressed. Even a little will go a long way and can be so helpful in boosting morale. Even if you're not the boss, try it with your colleagues and see how much better people feel about themselves.

Another aspect of self-esteem and relating to others is when you compare yourself with others, leading to internal rivalries at work. There may be jealousy, feeling someone's getting something that you deserve. So make sure that you are noticed by all means, be high-profile, yet also build your self-esteem and let go of resentment, focusing on yourself and your abilities rather than wasting any time in putting another person down.

Sometimes you may feel low self-esteem because you feel another person, maybe someone close to you at work, is not paying enough attention to you or putting their appreciation in the direction of someone else. You may want to be sure you have their loyalty. While it's appropriate to expect to come first with a spouse, at work you may get attention and support yet you cannot expect to have emotional support all the time.

Who is responsible for how *you* feel?

In truth, only you can be emotionally responsible for yourself. No other person can do it for you nor is it appropriate for you to be the emotional caretaker of any other person. You can't be responsible for how they're feeling all the time, nor can you make them happy. Whether it's your boss or a colleague, to attempt to do this will drain your energy and affect your self-esteem, especially if they seem unwilling to do much to help themselves. You will want to be kind to other people, yet you cannot ensure or be responsible for their state of mind. Each individual needs to do that for himself or herself. It will lower your self-esteem and energy if you're constantly trying to do this for another individual.

From your own point of view, it's better if you're able to do this for yourself, that is, be able to boost your own self-esteem. Then you can clearly ask for what you want rather than demanding it and needing it to keep your self-esteem high. This is the difference between loving to have approval, appreciation, support or asking for it on a professional basis and, on the other hand, being desperate, which is never an attractive proposition!

Self-respect and respect for others

For improved relationships, what you're aiming at is to treat everyone well and with respect, including yourself. This is not in any way to suggest that you are falsely nice yet unfair to yourself. The clearer you are about what's appropriate for you, the more clearly you can ask for what you want and the easier you will find it to give a high level of attention to colleagues and customers.

Self-esteem boosters

- Remember to express appreciation daily to colleagues, especially of a job well done.
- Let go of resentment when you notice it creeping in.
- What can *you* do to help a situation at work, where there is a challenge, perhaps misunderstandings?
- To promote harmony and co-operation, set mutual goals with high self-esteem thoughts.

Keynote booster

Keynote boosters can be used for a day or more, then use another booster of your choice.

Take a minute ... several times today to focus on the word *harmony* and what that means to you at work. What is one step you can take to create greater harmony at work?

5

JUST A WORD ... ABOUT CRITICISM

Bring Self-Esteem Into The Picture

Criticism without taking self-esteem into account can be unhelpful, both for the giver and the receiver. When your work is being criticized, particularly when appreciation has not been forthcoming, it can be difficult to feel valued for your overall contribution. Let yourself feel your feelings, let go of them, integrate them. That is, relax, feel them, they'll change. It is helpful to do this at home or at least on your own. You may also want to let off steam by confiding in a trusted friend or partner outside the work environment.

Then look objectively at what is being said, stall for time rather than reacting right away. Be willing to do what's appropriate if what is suggested is an improvement and not making unreasonable demands on you.

The importance of self-esteem

When your self-esteem is high you are less likely to feel demoralized and you'll also be able to make your case more clearly. So many of these issues are about personalities, power play, not about deciding objectives and meeting them. If you have a boss or a colleague with a problem, you may experience daily carping as a result of *their* low self-esteem. It's especially difficult with those who, through low self-esteem, drive themselves without respect and do the same to others! So keep your self-esteem high and look for ways in which you can improve your situation. Get support to improve things, both within the company and perhaps by looking outside it.

Communicate clearly and with compassion

When you want to put your point across, some reflection will help you identify what it is appropriate for you to say so you can do so more clearly and with respect for yourself and the other person or people.

When you want to communicate your feelings about another's actions or lack of them, be specific: 'when you . . . I feel . . .' or if you don't want to reveal your feelings, 'when you do x, y happens . . .'. For example, you might say either:

> 'I feel hurt when you don't support me at meetings' or 'When you don't support me at meetings we look like a weak team'.

You can ask for what you'd like to happen or the other person to do and say why. You can use persuasion by tying in what you see as the results of their compliance or the reverse. Try to avoid making it too much like a threat or a promise! For example:

'I'd like us to support each other then we can gain more backing from other Sections.'

Self-esteem needs to come into the picture with all communications at work. It is not being too aggressive or passive and, above all, it is being appropriate to the situation. Notice if you often put down yourself and others. Whether you feel your comments are justified or not, that is always going to bring your own energy down.

As well as taking appropriate action, reframe what you want to say in a more positive way and that will immediately help. From a point of self-esteem, don't get off-balance, off-centre, by matching energy if you have to deal with an angry person. Communicate clearly and with compassion.

Goodwill

From a self-esteem angle, always look at what is the intention behind your communication. It would be very different if it was to put down a person, make them wrong or to come up with a harmonious solution. If you're in the position of seeing another person every day or regularly at work, you will need to aim for a harmonious relationship with them. This does not mean you need to have lunch with them once a week or drinks after work, yet do all you can to seek to dissolve the animosity. Do this by working on your self-esteem and dissolving it within yourself first. With goodwill, all communications, even 'criticisms', go better.

The quality of your relationship with the person or other people involved will always be there as an important factor. For self-esteem, we can decide that we will communicate in a way that promotes ongoing harmonious relationships, trust and co-operation.

Self-esteem boosters

- What specifically makes you feel a particular way or results in certain circumstances? Be specific: 'when you do ... I feel ...' not 'Oh, you always do ...'.
- What do you want? What would you prefer the other person to do? Again, don't expect others to read your mind.
- What benefits would come from a change in behaviour, actions, attitude or what would be a disadvantage in not making this change?
- Can you express what you want to say more clearly and more compassionately?
- What other steps can you take to move forward, refocusing on yourself?

Notice there will be many times that our communication doesn't meet the ideal, so relax, let yourself off the hook.

Keynote booster

Keynote boosters can be used for a day or more, then use another booster of your choice.

Take a minute ... several times today to check the *clarity* and *compassion* of all your communications – ask 'Is this true?' and 'Is this helpful?'

6

SPOTLIGHT ON YOU!

Self-Esteem For Interviews, Meetings, Pay-Rise Requests And Presentations

Does a lack of self-esteem let you down at interviews and meetings? Do you back out of giving presentations? Are you too scared to ask for a pay-rise? In any situation where you feel you are being 'judged' by others, it is important to be able to raise the level of your self-esteem.

It's also important to attend to external factors and I would refer you to some of the excellent books in this series for that. However, it's equally important to prepare yourself on an *inner* level. So to make sure you are confident, the most important thing to bring in is *self-approval*. You can learn to, not boast, but maintain a steady confidence that sits lightly on you, as this is what will be picked up from you by others.

Your inner image

Your *inner image* is all you think and feel about yourself.

Raising your self-esteem will help you to feel better about any challenging situation. Also when you're feeling less than confident about yourself, this is going to be picked up by others, however glossy your exterior may be. And anyway, why suffer within yourself when boosting your self-esteem can assist you in getting through the situation graciously, perhaps even enjoyably?

Meetings

Preparation as to the purpose and content of the meeting is going to be very helpful to you. Yet preparation on an inner level is also very practical, to give you the confidence to show what you know. There's nothing more infuriating, as you may already have experienced, than not having the confidence to speak up with what you know or your ideas and then have someone else put them forward. So as well as knowing what you want to say and how it fits into the scheme of things, it's having the confidence to do this.

Bring in self-approval. Work daily on your self-esteem, not just right before the meeting. Practise, out loud to yourself, how you will make your main points and counter any criticisms calmly and with confidence.

While your role will determine your behaviour to a certain extent – whether you're head of a company, a manager, chairing the meeting, or you have just started at a junior level – what you have to say is important and deserves to be heard.

Appraisals

Appreciation is often forgotten! Appreciation of a person's good points is played down by some organizations, which isn't encouraging. If you're 'receiving' an appraisal, prepare for the meeting. Don't over-react, nor of course accept put-downs or sign statements that are unfounded. Whether you're the giver or receiver, remember to respect yourself and the other person, then it's easier to agree and act on recommendations without ill-feeling.

Asking for a pay-rise

Depending on what was said at your appraisal, this may be the right time to ask about a pay-rise. Certainly do it well before salary reviews. Do some research. Know the wage structure, and the way employees are ranked. Make sure you approach the right person when you ask for more money – responsibility might be with either personnel or management, so get the right one.

Then prepare yourself. It's very important to build up a sense of self-value. You have to have outward evidence that you are an achiever, but on a more subtle level you need self-esteem – you need to have an *'inner CV'* of the good qualities and abilities you have. There mustn't be a flicker of doubt in your mind, or it will be like trying to sell something when you have a sneaking suspicion about its value. So check how you think of yourself – if you are beset by self-doubt, just gently change your thoughts around. Negative thoughts can impede your progress and even stop you asking for your rise, so convert them into helpful ones. It's also really helpful if you can learn to integrate your emotions – recognize what you're feeling, let them move and change. Don't bottle up feelings like fear of asking for more money, anger at not being offered it, or even desperation. If you do, they may well be present in the actual conversation you have with the relevant person and experienced by them as 'negativity'.

If you are told 'no', find out if it's simply because you've asked at the wrong time. Ask to talk further. Try to avoid closing on a 'no'. You may need to persist – subtly, so they don't disappear when they see you approaching.

It's also important to consider that if you're doing a lot and not getting recognition your next pay-rise may be with another company!

Presentations

Have the self-esteem to *prepare*, whether you have two months or two minutes. Focus on the content and the ways of putting your message across that are appropriate to your audience. However, you also need to prepare by building self-esteem, so you have the confidence to be flexible should that be required and the confidence to deal with questions, challenges even. If you can do this without a hint of controlled anger or becoming defensive or aggressive, that will help you. Any edge is likely to be picked up by your audience.

Remember, however immaculate your appearance and argument, people want someone they can trust, someone who has confidence in themselves!

Practise your self-esteem. How as a person with self-esteem will you speak, walk in, conduct yourself in this important situation? See this in your mind's eye as you relax and imagine the scene.

Interviews

There will be outer preparation of your application, CV, research on the company and the position for which you are applying. Yet your *'inner CV'* is equally important – your thoughts and feelings about yourself, your own estimation of yourself. You can't expect other people to be fully accepting and approving of you if you don't feel that way about yourself! So work on those self-esteem boosters!

As part of your preparation for interviews, bring in your recognition of your good qualities and abilities. Have an appreciation of what you have to offer that is special. What will you bring that is unique to this job? Make a list that you can refer to and add to, then relax. Trust that if you do your preparation and give a confident response, and if this is the right job for you, you will get it.

If you're going for an interview after having been made redundant, it's especially important to remember that you're still of great value, regardless of your current status. So don't judge yourself as not being of value. Work then on building your self-esteem, know your market value but also know and be able to demonstrate your worth and value. Feel sure of that within yourself.

Going for and getting interviews for jobs you don't want for the 'experience' won't necessarily boost your self-esteem and may waste a considerable amount of your time. For an interview, although you can prepare questions you think you will be asked, when things go differently you may feel thrown. So when you're not asked what you expected or feel it's going badly, thinking, 'I've blown it', don't despair and let your self-esteem shrink. Instead, relax, bring your self-approval back so you can centre yourself. Muster your resources to get back in the flow of the interview and do yourself credit!

Self-esteem boosters

- Practise bringing in self-approval so you can experience that at will.
- Practise relaxing when you feel nervous so that this becomes your new response.
- Once again remind yourself of your good qualities, abilities and times when you've been successful.

- Practise some of what you'll say and repeat those things with confidence.
- Bring in self-esteem thoughts to boost your self-esteem, both before your interview, meeting or presentation, and during it.

Keynote booster

Keynote boosters can be used for a day or more, then use another booster of your choice.

Take a minute ... several times today as you prepare for an important event to do your *inner preparation* – that is, boost your self-esteem.

7

BUFFER STRESS WITH SELF-ESTEEM

Boosting Your Self-Esteem Helps Control Stress

Low self-esteem as a stressor

Research shows that low self-esteem is the biggest cause of stress. Low self-esteem thoughts bring your energy down – thoughts like, 'I knew this would happen', 'I'll never be able to', 'I can't', 'I'm nowhere near good enough', 'other people manage better'. When we feel bad about ourselves and under pressure, it makes it more difficult to perform at work or to move forward. The first step is to get those self-esteem thoughts in place. That will lift your energy and make it easier to centre yourself to do what needs to be done.

The best use of your time

With regard to controlling stress, look at what you can

achieve and actually do. Take a moment to reflect from a point of self-esteem, that is, to listen to yourself with regard to the best use of your time and energy. This will save you time and energy, perhaps a considerable amount of it. You can see more clearly what you need to do and you may also have some more understanding of your situation. Remember, in times of stress, to be extra gentle rather than harsh towards yourself and others, both in how you think and speak and how you treat yourself and them.

Of course pressures can come from all directions at the same time. There are times when many people have high expectations. It can be difficult to stay focused and complete what needs to be done, even when you want to. Feeling that you're wasting your time, trying to accomplish too many things is a sure way to create stress. You can reverse this by working on your self-esteem. Learn to relax. Identify what is important, both in what you need to achieve and the steps you need to take to do so. Then you can prioritize activities whether you will be doing them or by delegating them.

Keep your energy level high

You can look after your energy by keeping the level of your self-esteem high. Part of this will be listening to and monitoring what is important to you as you go about your business. When you feel better about yourself, you're also more likely to play your full part in the proceedings or project.

If *you* don't look after yourself, for example by preventing yourself getting over-strained and over-tired, no one else is going to! The quality of your contribution and your ability to sustain this will be helped by your looking after yourself – that is self-esteem in practice. Self-care is good for business and particularly noticeable when customer service is vital to your work. *You can give an extra-special service and quality of attention to others only when you know how to maintain your self-esteem on a daily basis.*

When you start to drive yourself, check if it's important to to be engaged in those activities. If it is, then perhaps take more frequent rests if you are tired, stopping earlier to do something completely different. You will be able to complete work of a higher quality in a shorter time if you do this and look after your energy.

You are unique

Low self-esteem and stress can come from ignoring both your intuition, that is, your hunches about what to do and what is best for you, and your individuality. The two are linked. Only you can determine what is appropriate for you as an individual – you are unique. If you are trying to build your life on someone else's 'shoulds', you will experience stress and frustration.

Start to get to know yourself by listening to your own intuition and desires. You know best what *is* right for you.

Practical relaxation

Taking time to learn to relax your body totally is another excellent way to control stress. You need to be on your own, sitting or lying down comfortably. Put on some relaxing music if you like or else have total peace and quiet. Then gently relax your body, your head to your toes, tensing each part and then relaxing it if that is better for you. Keep your breathing relaxed. Let go of any busy thoughts and pull your attention back to you. Focus on pleasant, helpful thoughts and good feelings. Picture pleasant outcomes to various situations. Take 10–20 minutes on this. Then take a moment before gently opening your eyes. Wait another minute before gently getting up.

As you get used to what it feels like to be relaxed, you will become more aware of when you're *starting* to get stressed. You will find it easier to immediately bring in a feeling of relaxation.

Letting go of fear

Fear is a great sapper of self-esteem and a stressor. Self-doubt and fear leave little room for self-esteem. You're also likely to use your time and energy, not in ways that help the situation but which pull down your self-esteem. When your self-esteem needs a boost because you're feeling fear over the future or remorse over the past, let go of any fear you have been feeling. Determine that you will use your energy to take a leap forward from negativity to helping yourself even more. Relax as you do this, so that you come from determination not desperation.

Other people as stressors!

When you're experiencing fear and low self-esteem thoughts, you will be at your most stressed. If part of what is tiring you is being with people you find draining, then keep relaxing when you're with them yet don't allow your time with them to continue any longer than is necessary. You may also feel extra sensitive to other people's demands, opinions and criticisms. While doing what you need to with regard to your work and personal responsibilities, you need to draw back, at least in your mind, from people who seem unsupportive or 'too much' right now.

Bring balance into your life – make time for *you*

If you've become low through a period of over-work or with worrying about changes, job security and prospects, then while continuing to acknowledge the importance of this, practise daily relaxation. Remembering to be extra gentle with yourself, schedule in at least one thing you enjoy each day, even 15 minutes of time for *you* works wonders.

People report that giving that 15 minutes to something they enjoy is a great self-esteem booster. To reduce stress and boost your self-esteem, don't delay in giving time also to personal relationships, even if you're very busy. Then you can create more *balance in your life*, more of what you want. You'll be boosting your self-esteem and as you boost your self-esteem, you get in an upward cycle, spiralling upwards. You can then give to yourself and those who are important to you more of what makes you flourish!

Self-esteem boosters

- Be persistent in changing unhelpful thought patterns and in reinforcing a helpful way of thinking. Learn to recognize your emotions. Accept and experience them so they cause less stress and exhaustion.
- Take a minute to stop and check that you're treating yourself and others with respect when you and they may be feeling fraught.
- Learn the steps to practical relaxation and do some daily.
- Check your life-style is in balance; it's important to make time for friends, family and creative interests. Take a moment to put 'dates' in your diary and keep to them.
- Do not be afraid to ask for support from family and friends or advice from professionals. Make a note of those who can help you and arrange to see them

informally or by making an appointment. Your first step is that telephone call!

- Look for something extra, however small, you really enjoy doing each day. Remember to treat yourself gently.

Keynote booster

Keynote boosters can be used for a day or more, then use another booster of your choice.

Take a minute ... several times today to have any stress remind you to relax your body totally, let go and say to yourself 'all *is* well'.

8

WORK CHOICES AND CHANGES

The Right Work For *You* Is A Must For Self-Esteem

Shape your future

We spend so much time at work that you owe it to yourself from a point of self-esteem, if your work isn't currently satisfying, to find out if there is work that would be more suited to you, that you could enjoy and where you can make your best contribution. If you consistently feel you're wasting your time in the job you're in, maybe you are! Ongoing low self-esteem is linked with dissatisfaction at work. Have the courage to find out what would be satisfying and joyful for you and move towards that.

With the rapid pace of change at work you may not feel in charge of decisions made about your job. With self-esteem, however, you can be in charge of the way you act and react. You are in charge of *shaping the future for yourself.*

A heart-search for a job-search!

Having the intention to and actively looking for the right job for you may mean looking within yourself as well as at the job market, that is, a heart-search as well as a job-search. If you do this while still in your current job, you may experience less of the uncertainty of not having a job. It is an opportunity to have the project of finding the right job for you, in your own time, that is for *you* as an individual with your unique qualities and requirements. It's worth spending time on this.

The self-esteem to go for it!

While in your current job, you also need to raise the level of your energy and your self-esteem. Then you can use that self-esteem to act as a springboard for moving forward into the right work for you.

When you feel you are in 'the wrong job', it is difficult to provide more than, at best, an 'adequate' service for others. The best work is done by those in a job that's right for them and this is particularly noticeable in the service industries. You may have experienced a time in your working life when your job felt like a drag, when it was all you could do to get yourself to work and through your workload, never mind quality attention to yourself, colleagues or customers!

Remember your value and worth

Very often our self-esteem is low when we realize that the nature of the work we're doing will not change and it's not something we now enjoy. Sometimes work that was appropriate for us at one time may no longer be so, say, five years later. Being in the wrong job relentlessly with no sign of change will have an effect on your self-esteem. Being without a job, especially for a long period of time, will also affect your self-esteem. Regardless of your current job status, even if you're in a job you don't like, even if you've been made redundant or are a young person who's finding difficulty getting the right job, *you are of great value and your contribution is important*. It's essential to remind yourself of this daily.

If you consistently stay in a job you don't like, without the motivation of a sense of achieving more, that is, of larger purpose, your self-esteem and well-being will continue to suffer.

Making the best of a bad job

While it's not usually appropriate to change jobs suddenly or to leave a job you don't like, while you look for something better, it's well worth thinking if there's a way of making your current job better before you go for a major change. That in itself will boost your self-esteem.

Notice the benefits of your current job, especially if you feel you have to look very hard for them! Even if it's one of those jobs where nothing is as good as leaving it. It will help your self-esteem to feel that you've made the best job that you could.

Could you make more of a contribution or are you putting in too much work and needing to, for example, leave work earlier to get on with things you love to do? This may be a hobby, time for yourself, enjoying yourself with family and friends.

It may be that other things like making small changes to your work area, taking a lunch break with food you enjoy, wearing clothes you look good in to work, help to tide you over. Sometimes doing what you can to create harmony with another person you've been having difficulty with can make things bearable.

Rather than feeling it doesn't matter because you know you're leaving anyway, boost your self-esteem to aim for this harmony. *Then you can carry goodwill with you to the next job.*

Redundancy

Sometimes you may be in the position of having to make a job change because you have been made redundant. Not much of a choice! You may well experience strong feelings about the way you've been treated. It's easy then to undervalue yourself. Bring in a sense of self-esteem. Remember you *are* of value, you have all your special qualities and abilities regardless of your job status. Remind yourself that you can get a job that is right for you and let go of upset feelings. Be determined and focus on finding work that is appropriate for you. Treat yourself gently and build up your energy to persevere with your job-search. Have faith in yourself and your ability to succeed. Be open to opportunities!

The right job for you

While in your current job, have as a personal project the aim of finding work you enjoy. You may know what you want. If not, by all means take psychometric tests, careers counselling, read books on different types of work and visit different organizations you feel would be appropriate. Yet, be aware that the main indicator is a self-esteem one, that is, when you do or even imagine yourself doing this activity, this type of work, do you feel better about yourself, do you feel a sense of energy, purpose, a sense of joy?

Start from what you enjoy. You can tell when you feel more enthusiastic, lighter, more joyful, that you are moving in the right direction.

Sometimes an activity you regard as a hobby will take an

important place in your life. You will realize that you want to spend more and more time on it. Perhaps it's something you make or a service you could receive payment for. As you boost your self-esteem, you will realize that in due course you will be set to make money from doing work you enjoy.

The bigger picture

You need to look at the bigger picture. Where do you want to be in five/ten/twenty years' time? *This is a self-esteem issue!* Regard this as important enough to find out and start today, even in the 30 minutes you have to reflect on this.

What do you want to achieve? What would you hate not to achieve? Bring in self-esteem and personal intuition to keep discovering what is appropriate for you so you can set goals and take action. Bring in self-esteem at all times for self-motivation, to get started, to persevere and complete each stage of your exciting journey.

Self-esteem boosters

- Brush up skills you want to improve, for example for interviews or having a greater facility with IT.
- Support your success by keeping self-esteem thoughts to the forefront of your mind like 'I can do this', 'I'm building on the success I already have', 'I now deserve to have work I love'.
- Back up your self-esteem thoughts by letting go of any feelings of self-blame or blaming others.
- Consider further training. Is that going to be necessary? Find out!
- Expand the network of people who know you're in the job market. Consider attending meetings of professional

associations, conferences, local business associations as well as telling friends, family, colleagues and former colleagues.

- Have this as your most important project, *the right work for you*. Keep notes daily of your ideas and practical steps to take.

Keynote booster

Keynote boosters can be used for a day or more, then use another booster of your choice.

Take a minute ... several times today to reflect both on how you can improve your current job situation and on how you can move towards the ideal work for *you*.

9

SELF-ESTEEM TREATMENT

Pay Attention To What You Need

Look after yourself

You boost your self-esteem by paying attention to what you need to do to keep yourself feeling good. Because it is your responsibility to do this, not another person's, that puts you in a position of *power and independence*. It also means you don't blame others or any other person in particular for your feeling bad, low self-esteem or out of sorts with yourself!

While you won't want to accept behaviour that's rude or inappropriate, you don't need other people to behave in a certain way so that you may feel good. Now that's a relief. What freedom for them and for you, what a self-esteem boost!

Treating yourself better – what can you do?

Treating yourself well does include being vigilant with regard to your mind, not allowing yourself to focus on thoughts that are hurtful or irrelevant to you. It's also not wasting your time on things that are not important. You can use your time on matters that are important to you, yet in a way that's enjoyable. You might want to stop and ask yourself right now 'What is the most important use of my time today?'

Self-esteem treatment is caring for yourself on all levels. With regard to your body, it may be giving yourself enough rest and relaxation, enough exercise, grooming, nice coloured clothes or treatments, foods that nurture you and that you enjoy eating. You've got to eat, dress and groom yourself anyway so it may just as easily be in a way that enhances your self-esteem as not!

What self-esteem treatment can you give your body this week? You may be able to think of several. However, spending 15–30 minutes on something this week may be more satisfying than a longer time further into the future, helping you to start now to treat your body well. Then look at treating yourself better in other ways.

- Can you treat yourself better with regard to enhancing your closest relationship? Can you make that more intimate and romantic or whatever it is you want for yourself?
- With regard to friends and family, have you got the balance of those who are supportive, with those who you spend a great deal of time supporting? Are there people you'd love to spend time with? When can you make arrangements?
- With regard to treating yourself better in terms of your home or work environment, are there ways you can

improve that, make it more pleasurable by keeping things tidy, bringing in more fresh flowers, plants and pictures?

Self-esteem treatment is looking after yourself in all aspects. It's particularly important to treat yourself gently when the pressure is on. Be aware that treating yourself well from a self-esteem point of view goes beyond indulging yourself or giving yourself treats.

Your deeper needs

Looking after yourself, treating yourself well, is not just caring for your immediate physical and personality needs. You will always have more desires: that is part of the mechanism that moves us forward. To treat yourself really well, from a self-esteem perspective, you need to pay attention to your deeper needs which will be personal to you as an individual.

Sometimes satisfaction comes from working later to complete a project or piece of work that is important to you. At other times it comes from stopping work early to do something completely different. Only you can decide this for yourself.

Find out what is joyful and important to you

What is important to you and what gives you joy may be very different from what is appropriate for any other person. It can also take you time to find out what is important for you to accomplish long term as well as on a daily basis. You may also need to reflect on what gives you joy. This is very personal to you and may vary from time to time. *Respecting yourself in this way will provide a lasting boost to your self-esteem.*

Self-esteem boosters

- Think of one way you could do something that gives you joy, that's pleasing to you and make the time to do it.
- Don't torture or hurt yourself by saying or thinking 'unkind' things about yourself or others. Let go and focus on what you now want to create in your life.
- Listen to yourself, to how you are feeling. Do what is necessary to get your body feeling good and your energy higher.
- Treat yourself well with regard to how you spend your time and energy, daily and long term. Think of one way you can treat yourself better in each area of your life and make plans to put that in place.

Keynote booster

Keynote boosters can be used for a day or more, then use another booster of your choice.

Take a minute ... several times today to ask 'What can I do for myself this week that is enjoyable?' Put a date and a time in your diary to do it.

10

SET GOALS WITH SELF-ESTEEM

For Plans You Really Follow Through

Wake up to what you want

Low self-esteem is tied in with low aspirations. This is when you have no significantly important goals for yourself on a professional or a personal basis. With a boosted level of self-esteem it may be time to wake up and consider what you do want for yourself! It can be a vicious circle. Because of low self-esteem, you don't think or feel that you're worthy or capable of achieving or receiving very much. So you don't set goals that are important and meaningful to you. There follows dissatisfaction and further low self-esteem!

The cycle continues until you do decide to boost your self-esteem by choosing helpful thoughts, by caring for and respecting yourself enough to listen to yourself. This is with regard to what is important to *you* and joyful for you to achieve.

You know what is best for *you*

Having the self-esteem to listen to yourself includes giving attention and time to consider your hunches with regard to goals that are right for *you*. It means that you listen to yourself with regard to steps that are appropriate for you to take. It is this listening to the whispers in your mind, to elements of your dreams and daydreams, to your hunches, as well as having a relaxed yet alert consideration of what it is appropriate for you at any time. Reflecting on choices from a point of self-esteem is more likely to lead you to goals that will be truly satisfying and that you will want to follow through.

The right goals for you

So take a few minutes to pay attention to this daily or at least on a regular basis. Then you can formulate goals for things you truly want to achieve. While you will wish to bring into the picture, or even better, set mutual goals with friends, family and colleagues, you won't want, through low self-esteem, to take on the 'shoulds' of other people. For high self-esteem you need to put your time and energy into what you as an individual want to achieve. This is for both your long-term goals and daily objectives.

Outline the vital or essential aspects of your goal, or goals. For example, if you want to reorganize your garden and the most important thing is to have fragrance and vegetables, then work in the relevant parts first.

If you want a new job, look at exactly which aspects are most important. For some people, location will be a primary consideration. Others need to have plenty of people around them or the opportunity to use their creative skills.

Deciding what you want

Work out what is appropriate for you. If you want more fun, what does that mean to you? This can vary enormously from one person to another!

Obviously some goals will be easier to achieve than others. Write out goals as clearly as you can, putting in a time frame – one year, six months, three months, one month, one week, or whatever you choose. What do you have as your most important goal for yourself through the next year, six, or three months? If it's a job, for example, you may want to be settled in a new one and to have set up appropriate training within a year. You may want to have set up interviews within six months. You may want to have clarified exactly what you want within three months or even one month. You can speed up the time frame to fit in with what you want.

Self-esteem supports your success

When you're focusing on what is appropriate to you, another thing to remember are your self-esteem thoughts. You need to have appropriate thoughts as well as setting goals. There's no point in having goals you want for yourself and then telling yourself, 'I'll never manage to do this', 'I'm not good enough'. Change your thoughts to 'I am good enough to do this', 'I'm making progress'. From a self-esteem angle, think about who will be supportive of you, someone or more than one person who has your best interests at heart or who has just achieved what you want to do or who simply can be of professional assistance to you. Then just reflect on practical steps you need to take. Planning one of them as something you can do in the next week means that you take a first step right away.

Unless you give yourself what you really want at a deep

level, dissatisfaction, resentment and low self-esteem will continue. Rather than goals you feel you 'should' have, goals that are dear to your heart, important to you as an individual, will be the goals that you will want to follow through.

Self-esteem boosters

- Listen to yourself and then keep a note of hunches, dreams, ideas and thoughts on your project.
- Write out your goals clearly with time frames, perhaps one year, six months, three months and one month.
- Add self-esteem thoughts to support your goals, for example 'I know what I want to achieve', 'I can do this', then use your own most helpful thoughts.
- Look at what needs to be changed or improved. Make a step-by-step plan to tackle this.
- Who will support you? Are there people who can be supportive of you in achieving this goal?
- What is a step you can take right now to move forward?
- Review your goals, spending a short time on them each week. Take one at a time, then even a few minutes planning will be well spent.

Keynote booster

Keynote boosters can be used for a day or more, then use another booster of your choice.

Take a minute ... several times today to ask yourself of different activities – 'How does this fit in with today's most important goal for myself?'

'PICK ME UP' PAGE

However well prepared and confident we are, there will always be people and situations that tend to throw us. All you have learnt in the book will help you to deal with the strong emotions you may experience. However, for a quick boost in a crisis:

- Take a deep breath, relax your body, remind yourself 'I can handle this'.
- Get away from the situation or person on your own if you can, even for a short time. This may mean walking around the block or at least to the loo if that's at work.
- Experience your feelings and let them go. If you can't do this now because you're at work, set aside a time later when you know you will do this and keep to it.
- Bring in self-esteem thoughts, supportive thoughts about yourself and the situation, for example 'I can handle this'/'I believe in myself'.
- Talk to someone you trust to get it out of your system or write it out.
- As you relax a little and centre yourself, become aware of what's the most appropriate step for you to take.
- Remind yourself this is a situation that you're *going through* and you will come through it!

- Do something enjoyable for yourself today to give yourself a break from the situation.
- Keep letting go and bringing in self-esteem thoughts.
- Listen to yourself with regard to appropriate steps and get support from friends on this.

FINALE

Boosting your self-esteem is about getting back in balance, having all aspects of your life work together for you. Self-esteem thoughts with appropriate actions give you more joy and satisfaction in your life. Self-esteem on an emotional level works by your letting yourself feel your feelings, whatever they are, so that they change and flow, then you're not stuck with your anger, resentment and fear. It also works when you bring in feelings of having everything working out well. Remember, you can bring in those good feelings when you choose.

It's very important to have that 15 minutes of time just for you each day, however you want to use it, so long as it's something you enjoy. It's space and time for you. People report greater self-esteem and satisfaction when they give themselves even a small amount of time, especially when they're very busy. By satisfying the 'what about me?' part of you, you're satisfying yourself. Then you're more likely to want to satisfy other people, which is particularly important with regard to work colleagues and customers.

While you can continue your self-esteem building further through programmes – either public or for your organization – you already have the basis for boosting your self-esteem whenever you want to use it.

Perhaps the biggest boost to your self-esteem is knowing that you *can* boost your own self-esteem! Then while you may be apparently 'dependent' on other people for some of the material aspects of your life and, with regard to work, if you have a boss to 'answer' to, you will still have *inner independence*. This in itself makes the process valuable and worthwhile.

Once you've read this book through and put those suggestions that appeal to you into practice, you'll have a greater sense of *strength* and *freedom* as a result of *boosting your self-esteem*.

Take a minute ... or even 30, to look at what you now want for yourself and in your life. Believe in yourself. You can do it. You have the rest of your life ahead of you. With higher self-esteem so much more is possible!

FURTHER INFORMATION

If you would like to find out more about Patricia Cleghorn's work, you may be interested in programmes by Orchid International, for people in organizations and The Self-Esteem Company, with courses for the public. Please contact:

Patricia Cleghorn, Principal
Orchid International, The Self-Esteem Company
PO Box 354
London, W13 9NU
Tel: 44 (0)1491 875135
email: orchid2100@aol.com